WS

WS

PICTURE A COUNTRY

# Italy

Henry Pluckrose

**W**
FRANKLIN WATTS
LONDON•SYDNEY

This is the Italian flag.

First Published in 1998
by Franklin Watts
This edition 2001

Franklin Watts
96 Leonard Street
London EC2A 4XD

Franklin Watts Australia
56 O'Riordan Street
Alexandria, Sydney
NSW 2015

© Franklin Watts 1998

ISBN 0 7496 4287 4

A CIP catalogue record for this book is
available from the British Library

Dewey Decimal Classification Number: 914.5

10 9 8 7 6 5 4 3 2 1

Series Editor: Rachel Cooke
Designer: Kirstie Billingham
Picture research: Juliet Duff

Printed in Great Britain

Photographic acknowledgements:

Cover: Top Getty Images (Simeone Huber),
middle (Chris Windsor), bottom (Hideo Kurihara).

AA Photo Library p. 10 both;
AKG, London pp. 27, 29 (Erich Lessing);
Camera Press p. 17 (Ben Coster);
Cephas Picture Library p. 13 (Mick Rock);
Colorsport p. 25 both;
James Davis Travel Photography pp. 8, 11;
Ferrari p. 16;
Getty Images pp. 9 (Hans Peter Merten),
12 (Simeone Huber), 14, 23 (Chris Windsor),
26 (Louis Grandadm), 28 (Hideo Kurihara);
Granata Press Service p. 20 (F. Annabali);
Robert Harding Picture Library pp. 15 (John Ross),
19 (Michael Short);
Hutchison Library p. 22 (Davey);
Performing Arts Library p. 24 (Gian Franco Fainello).

All other photography by Steve Shott.

Map by Julian Baker.

# Contents

# Where is Italy?

This is a map of Italy.

Italy is in Europe.

Italy is shaped like a boot.

At its toe is a large island called Sicily.

Here are some Italian stamps and money.

Italian money is called lire.

# The Italian landscape

Italy is a country of high mountains
and beautiful hills.
Its two main mountain ranges are
the Italian Alps and the Apennines.

In northern Italy and in the mountains,
the winter weather is cold.
In southern Italy even the winters are warm.
Summers in Italy are warm and mostly dry.

# The Italian people

People have lived in Italy
for many thousands of years.
Today over 57 million people
live in Italy.

Naples is the largest city in southern Italy.

The village of Rivello is built over high hills in Basilicata, a region in the south of Italy.

# Where they live

In the south of Italy, many people live in small towns and villages.

In northern Italy, most people live in large towns and cities, including Milan, Turin, Venice and Bologna.

This busy street is in Florence in northern Italy.

The Baraccia Fountain was built in 1627.
It is at the bottom of the Spanish Steps in Rome.

# The capital city

Rome is the capital of Italy.
It is built on 7 hills.
Nearly 3 million people live there.
Rome is a city of fine buildings,
squares, statues and fountains.

A legend tells that Rome was first
built by twins Romulus and Remus.
They were brought up by a she-wolf.

# Italian design

Italy is famous for its designers.
A designer is someone who decides
how things look.

Italians design fashionable clothes.
They also design attractive cars.

# Making wine

This is a picture of
a vineyard in Tuscany.
Italian farmers grow black
and white grapes.
They are used to make wine.

# Family and home

Italians spend a lot of time
with their families.

This family is shopping together. They are choosing
fresh fruit and vegetables from a local market stall.

This family will have spaghetti with grated cheese on top and salad for their evening meal.

Italians like to eat together as a family.
They may make their meal together as well.

# Italian food

Italians eat pasta, such as spaghetti,
with many of their meals.
They enjoy fish, hot and
cold meats, chicken and
salads soaked in oil and garlic.
They also make delicious ice-cream.

# Out and about

Italians enjoy going to the opera.
An opera is like a play,
but all the words are sung.

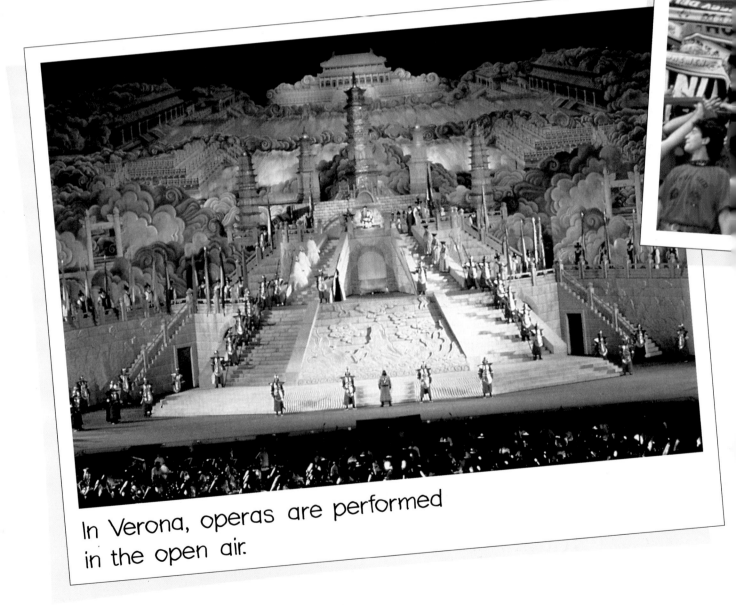

In Verona, operas are performed
in the open air.

On Sunday afternoons,
many Italians go to
watch football.

On special days, crowds gather in St. Peter's Square in the Vatican City to hear the Pope speak.

# The Pope

The Pope is the most important priest in the Roman Catholic Church. He lives in the Vatican City, close to the centre of Rome.

The leaning tower of Pisa is one of the most famous buildings in Italy.

# Visiting Italy

Many tourists like to visit Italy.
They go to look at its fine, old buildings,
and to visit its art galleries and museums.

These horses are statues
from St. Mark's cathedral
in Venice.

# Index

# About this book

The last decade of the 20th century has been marked by an explosion in communications technology. The effect of this revolution upon the young child should not be underestimated. The television set brings a cascade of ever-changing images from around the world into the home, but the information presented is only on the screen for a few moments before the programme moves on to consider some other issue.

Instant pictures, instant information do not easily satisfy young children's emotional and intellectual needs. Young children take time to assimilate knowledge, to relate what they already know to ideas and information which are new.

The books in this series seek to provide snapshots of everyday life in countries in different parts of the world. The images have been selected to encourage the young reader to look, to question, to talk. Unlike the TV picture, each page can be studied for as long as is necessary and subsequently returned to as a point of reference. For example, an Italian town might be compared with the one in their own local area; a discussion might develop about the ways in which food is prepared and eaten in a country whose culture and customs are different from their own.

The comparison of similarity and difference is the recurring theme in each of the titles in this series. People in different lands are superficially different. Where they live (the climate and terrain) obviously shapes the sort of houses that are built, but people across the world need shelter; coins may look different, but in each country people use money.

At a time when the world seems to be shrinking, it is important for children to be given the opportunity to focus upon those things which are common to all the peoples of the world. By exploring the themes touched upon in the book, children will begin to appreciate that there are strands in the everyday life of human beings which are universal.